CAREER BOOK 4
16 Career-readiness Strategies for Parents of College Students With Special Needs

JIM HASSE

DEDICATION

To my brother, Paul, who, during the 1970s, anticipated the impact
personal computers and cyberspace would have
on 21st century agriculture.

CONTENTS

Growing in Self-confidence

Discovering Disability's Competitive Advantage

ACKNOWLEDGMENTS

A special thank you to Peter Altschul, Fernando Botelho, Earl Brancel, Judy Ettinger, Floyd Harris, Pam Hasse, Nan Hawthorne, Mary Krohn, Nancy O'Connell, Liz Seger, Ruth-Ellen Simmonds, Don Storhoff, Mårten Tegnestam and Bob Williams – all of whom (among many others) have provided me with valuable guidance during critical moments in my career development.

WHAT I BELIEVE

Over the last 20 years, I have identified a range of time-tested strategies I believe parents can use to prepare youngsters with disabilities for the world of work.

I believe guiding parents in implementing these strategies on a wide scale will bring these two results:

- More people with disabilities will be ready for work.
- Employers will find more job candidates with disabilities who they consider qualified for open jobs.

That's why I seek non-profit and corporate partners which have wide, established connections with parents who are looking for the answers I can provide about how to help their youngsters with special needs prepare for meaningful careers.

My message: I believe people can put disability to work as a competitive edge in today's job market.

For a long time, those of us dealing with disability employment issues have realized that individuals with a disability can add a valuable perspective to corporate efforts in the mainstream business world.

That message has had a difficult time getting public attention, but that may be changing.

I believe we can now more confidently state this finding: Employees with disabilities are more likely to bring drive, focus and innovation to the workplace than their non-disabled counterparts.

Consider the following three contemporary authors who have recently brought those three "advantages" of disability employment to the public's attention through books which have received good reviews in the mainstream media.

First, in "The Triple Package: What Really Determines Success" (2014), Amy Chua and Jed Rubenfeld discuss the reasons behind personal achievement.

Successful people, they say, tend to feel simultaneously inadequate and superior. They:

1. Believe they are, in some ways, exceptional.
2. Are insecure about their worth or place in society – that they're not "good enough."
3. Resist the temptation to give up instead of persevering in the face of difficult circumstances.

They may appear to have a chip on their shoulders because they have a need to prove themselves.

For those of us with a disability, for instance, we may have a personal need to prove to others that we are the "exception" to commonly held beliefs within our society about people with disabilities in general.

I believe that inadequate/superior package tends to generate a personal drive in "overachieving" individuals with a disability – a need to prove oneself by sacrificing present gratification in pursuit of future attainment.

I must confess that this inadequate/superior duality fits me to a tee. For a thorough examination of that duality in me, go to the directory for my series of seven Amazon books about my personal transformation stories as a person with cerebral palsy at cerebral-palsy-career-builders.com/transformation-stories.html.

Second, Geoff Colvin sums up the power of deliberate practice with a purpose in his book, "Talent Is Overrated: What Really Separates World-Class Performers from Everybody Else" (2010). He writes:

> "...The most important effect of practice in great performers is that it takes them beyond -- or, more precisely, around – the limitations most of us think of as critical."

He pinpoints exactly why I believe it makes good business sense to hire people with disabilities who have developed the motivation to work hard at precisely the things they need to improve so they can contribute to a company's bottom line.

Colvin cites research that indicates what we think of as "innate talent" is more accurately termed "long-term, sustained practice at what really counts" driven by a passion to reach a goal (or in response to the triple package described above by Amy Chua and Jed Rubenfeld). In other words, Colvin says it's all about self-discipline no matter what the motivation.

Third, in "David and Goliath: Underdogs, Misfits and the Art of Battling Giants" (2013), Malcolm Gladwell offers a new interpretation of what it means to live well with a disability.

His main point: What is innovative, beautiful and important in the world often arises from what looks like suffering and adversity.

In other words, being an underdog can change people. "It can open doors and create opportunities and educate and enlighten and make possible what otherwise may seem unthinkable," Gladwell writes.

Gladwell even promotes the idea of a "desirable difficulty," such as dyslexia, a learning disability that causes much frustration for students as they learn how to read but, at the same time, forces them to compensate for that barrier by developing better listening and problem-solving skills – and by being innovative.

I encourage you, as a parent, to keep these considerations in mind as you help your youngster with special needs prepare for a meaningful job in an integrated work situation.

I researched and wrote the material for this book long before the afore-mentioned authors became popular. Over the last 20 years, I have gradually realized the importance of disability as the foundation for the resiliency of humankind throughout history.

However, only in the last five years have I publicly admitted that my disabilities, while they have made life tougher for me to live, have also, within certain contexts, become an aggregate advantage for me.

That reconciliation – and even love – of one's personal vulnerabilities perhaps come with age and the advantage of hindsight.

At any rate, please keep these initial remarks in mind as you review the following career-readiness strategies for your youngster. Your youngster's personal circumstances as well as the National Career Development Guidelines in the back of this book can also temper your thoughts.

Will your youngster be able to frame disability in such a way when he or she makes the transition from school to work that will help hiring managers recognize disability's competitive advantage?

Will those hiring managers seize the opportunity they have for boosting drive, focus and innovation in their workplaces by hiring your son or daughter?

I believe the answer to both of those questions can be "yes."

But, first things first. Your youngster needs to first grow in self-confidence.

STRATEGY 1 – USE THESE GUIDELINES TO CHOOSE A CAREER COUNSELOR

You are not your college student's career counselor.

You're acting as a mentor or advisor who is interested in exploring with him or her some of the deliberate steps which can help build a meaningful career.

In short, you're a guide. As a guide, you may wish to help your college student find an effective career counselor.

And, during that process, you may want to remind your youngster that you have a unique role, using language such as this:

> "Only you are in charge of your career. You are in an all-terrain vehicle, and you're in the driver's seat. You need to learn how to traverse today's job market on your own with feedback from me and a qualified career counselor."

Overall, a career counselor's goal, according to Richard N. Bolles, author of "What Color Is Your Parachute?," is to help your college student make choices in terms of career, job and workplace so he or she feels that:

- "What I do really matters."
- I'm fully tapping into my skills and attributes."
- "I'm growing in my particular field of endeavor."

In other words, a career counselor helps an individual get on a career path that is right for him or her.

A career counselor needs to be someone who:

- **Asks** "what" -- but never "why" questions -- and asks your college student to give supporting evidence for his or her claims about skills, attributes, interests etc.
- **Asks** "how," "when" and "who" to help your college student identify personal behaviors, breaking the process of self-examination down into small steps.
- **Gives** your college student homework and requires effort on his or her part as a "buy-in" into the process of self-examination and personal decision making because each individual, without knowing it, has most of the answers about how to build a career and, as a result, need to do most of the exploratory work involved.
- **Collaborates** with your college student in a personal dialogue (whether it be in person, via Skype or in real time chat) and figuratively sits in front of a mirror with your student to find who he or she is and can become -- a process which can help uncover hidden barriers and how to work around them.
- **Gives** your college student information about career options -- not what he or she personally needs as a counselor to further his or her own career.
- **Allows** your college student to make personal decisions and come up with leads for particular jobs.
- **Walks** your college student through the process of career development and job seeking.
- **Knows** how to challenge your college student as well as hold his or her hand while working through that career development process.
- **Encourages** your college student to work with two or three peers in challenging one another to find their paths to meaningful careers.
- **Is** familiar with your college student's field of study and is knowledgeable about the options available in the job market for his or her particular set of disciplines.

Beyond Bolles' 10 criteria, I'd recommend clarifying, in your mind, the options your college student has in choosing a career counselor. There are at least three types of career practitioners to consider. Let's take a brief look at each.

The three types are:

- Global Career Development Facilitator (GCDF).
- Career Counselor.
- Vocational Rehabilitation Counselor (VRC)

Global Career Development Facilitator (GCDF)

One of the more common places you'll find GCDFs in the U.S. is at Career One Stop Centers, which are sponsored by the U.S. Department of Labor. The GCDFs at centers like these mainly work with people who are making career transitions.

GCDF training is built around 12 core competencies identified by career counseling experts. A period of supervised career facilitation practice also is required prior to certification. The 12 competency areas addressed in GCDF training are these: helping skills, labor market resources, assessment, diversity, ethics, career development models, employability skills, training practices, program management, public relations, technology, and supervision.

The GCDF certification is managed by the Center for Credentialing & Education, which requires continuing education for GCDFs beyond the initial certification process.

GCDFs must have a bachelor's degree but are not career counselors. I have been a GCDF since 1995.

Career Counselor

Unlike GCDFs, career counselors are required to have a master's degree in counseling. They must demonstrate the knowledge and skills (which are similar to the GCDF competencies) for a specialty in career counseling that a generalist counselor might not possess.

After conducting a thorough evaluation of your college student's personality traits, counselors must use their expertise to help your youngster assess skills and identify careers where those skills may be most profitably employed, both financially and in terms of job satisfaction.

Counselors are responsible for knowing what skills are needed in a broad variety of professions, how much they pay, and what a hiring authority will want to see in a successful applicant.

They then coach your college student through the process of researching fields that match his or her interests, setting up informational interviews with people to supplement company research, and finally targeting or creating specific job positions that meet your college student's needs.

They can be employed by a secondary school or college or work as independent consultants or in job placement firms.

Vocational Rehabilitation Counselor (VRC)

Vocational rehabilitation counseling is focused on helping people who have disabilities achieve their personal, career, and independent living goals through a counseling process.

Before deciding whether to work with a vocational rehabilitation counselor (VRC) or a mainstream career counselor, your college student may find it helpful to answer these questions:

- Do I need special consideration of my special needs in determining a career path?
- Do I need to learn more about how assistive technologies might be used in certain job settings?
- Am I worried that the career center on campus may not know how to assess the impact of my special needs on my career choices?
- Am I concerned that a VRC may pigeonhole me into 'typical' disability jobs?
- Will I need training customized for my special needs in order to find or qualify for a position in my chosen career field?
- Might I need an advocate to stand behind me when talking to potential employers?

No matter how your college student answers any of these questions for choosing or not choosing a VRC, just raising the awareness of these concerns or possibilities can be a valuable exercise.

The only difference that should exist between a career counselor and a VRC is the number of specialized tools and the amount of information they have for accommodating special needs as your college student makes career decisions.

But, remember, a VRC is empowered to choose the level of accommodation expenditures on a case-by-case basis.

And a VRC will provide one service that other career professionals do not offer: information about, training with and (sometimes) funding for assistive technology.

And, remember: All three of these practitioners, not just a career counselor, require official accreditation. They are not to be confused with life coaches, business coaches, or executive coaches, who may not be trained or certified as career practitioners.

Overall, the secret to a great experience with a career practitioner boils down to examining the individual's credentials and approach, being clear about your college student's own goals, and working diligently under that person's guidance.

When your college student is willing to take responsibility for his or her career path and you both have reviewed the above guideposts, it's time to choose a career professional (a GCDF, career counselor or VRC) who is trained to help individuals make sound decisions which will lead to meaningful work.

Selecting the right career professional for your soon-to-graduate son or daughter is a step toward enhanced self-confidence.

STRATEGY 2 – HEED
REHAB COUNSELOR SURVEY RESULTS

A recent survey which involved the perceptions of job development professionals such as vocational rehab counselors provide your college student with some potential job seeker strategies to consider when he or she hits the job market.

In August 2011, TransCen reported findings on the attitudes and beliefs of job development professionals toward employers to the Heldrich Center for Workforce Development at Rutgers University.

The report is part of the New Jersey DiscoverAbility project, a Comprehensive Employment Services Medicaid Infrastructure Grant funded by the U.S. Department of Health and Human Services, Centers for Medicare and Medicaid Services to the New Jersey Department of Human Services and its management partner, the John J. Heldrich Center for Workforce Development at Rutgers.

Results of the report focused on the attitudes and beliefs of job development professionals, such as state vocational rehab counselors, toward employers and the employment process.

The study's sponsors sought to examine how those beliefs tend to shape the job development and placement practices of the New Jersey and Maryland professionals involved in a set of six two-hour focus groups (36 participants) and a web-based survey (260 participants).

The majority of the respondents (80 percent) to the web-based survey were employed in community rehabilitation programs, providing services to a diverse population of people with physical, mental and emotional disabilities.

Most of the vocational rehab respondents were female (74 percent), and the majority had at least a BA degree (61 percent). Almost 34 percent of the respondents had 10 or more years of experience in job development.

I found what the vocational rehab participants said about employers quite interesting -- although that was not the primary focus of the study.

For instance, consider the following nine snippets I've chosen to highlight from the overall results. Here's how the vocational rehab professionals in the survey responded. Those results can give your college student glues for building a "getting hired" strategy, one designed to convince targeted employers to "hire me."

- **86 percent** of the respondents agreed with this statement: "Employers with a history of hiring people with disabilities are more likely to hire my client."

  That tells me that targeting employers with proven track records of attracting, hiring and promoting people with disabilities should be a primary strategy.

- **74 percent** agreed that "employers base hiring decisions on the bottom line." 81 percent of respondents with five or more years of experience agreed with this statement compared to 65 percent for those with less than five years of experience.

  Said one respondent, "Employers who base hiring decisions on the 'bottom line' might just not believe in the work capacity of people with disabilities."

  As a job seeker, that would prompt me to look at my past accomplishments, identify my skills and attributes which made those situations successful and then put what I had achieved into bottom-line, quantifiable results.

You may want to guide your college student into doing the same.

- **69 percent** agreed that "employers are more likely to hire people with disabilities if they have entry-level positions."

  If I were just getting out of school, I would not hesitate to take an entry-level job (no matter how menial it may appear to be), if my research shows the company and its particular field have good long-term prospects. Getting in on the ground floor of a company which is likely to grow rapidly is a golden opportunity.

  That's another tip to pass on to your mentee.

- **68 percent** agreed that "employers need to be sold on hiring people with disabilities." 75 percent of respondents with five or more years of experience agreed with this statement compared to 67 percent for those with less than five years of experience.

  I would hone my "bottom-line" success stories and use them as the foundation for my job marketing campaign -- and practice telling them in a concise way during job interviews.

  I strongly recommend this strategy for your youngster with special needs.

- **67 percent** agreed with this statement: "Employers prefer to know in advance if an applicant has a disability."

  My "bottom-line" success stories would show how learning how to live well with my particular disability has helped me develop the skills and attributes that were vital in achieving those accomplishments.

  Your college student needs to think about how to best meet this employer expectation of knowing in advance about his or her special needs.

- **62 percent** agreed with this sentence: "Employers are less likely to hire people with disabilities in the current economy." 80 percent of respondents with five or more years of experience agreed with this statement compared to 58 percent for those with less than five years of experience.

  One respondent said, "I think a major barrier is the economy right now. Years ago, our clients wanted an entry-level job nobody wanted. Now, we are fighting to get these jobs."

  I would evaluate my field of study for future career prospects and commit myself to lifelong learning in a job sector where job demand outstrips supply of qualified candidates.

- **57 percent** agreed that "employers are reluctant to hire people with disabilities due to the perceived costs involved."

  Part of my "sales pitch" as a job seeker would be to talk about any accommodations I may need, the costs involved and how I could help minimize the time, work and costs of getting me up to speed as a new hire.

- **56 percent** agreed that "employers are likely to hire clients for volunteer jobs."

  I would volunteer, offer to work for free for the opportunity to show what I could do or take an internship without pay -- anything to get my foot in the door of the right company and make myself the exception to the common occurrence of "being the last to be hired."

- **52 percent** agreed the "employers with off-site HR mangers are less likely to hire people with disabilities."

  Unless I had an entrepreneurial spirit (and perhaps knew some buddies from college who were involved in start-up companies where I could also spread my wings), I would target companies with well-established HR and diversity programs (backed by third-party endorsements).

Three statements from vocational rehab counselors in the survey popped out for me because they received nearly even splits (and can be perceived as unconvincing reasons to hire your college student):

- **40 percent agreed, 30 percent were neutral and 30 disagreed** with this statement: "Small businesses are more likely to hire people with disabilities."
- **35 percent agreed, 40 percent were neutral and 25 disagreed** with this statement: "Employers are influenced to hire by available tax incentives."
- **32 percent agreed, 43 percent were neutral and 25 disagreed** with this statement: "Employers with high staff turnover are motivated to hire people with disabilities."

I would build my job search strategies around the first nine vocational rehab counselor findings above.

However, your college student may want to think twice about targeting a small business (unless he or she has an inside, trusted contact in the company), hyping the tax incentives a prospective employer may receive by hiring him or her and using the "I'll-stay-with-you" pitch as a retention benefit he or she may bring to the table.

I believe these little bits of insight from those in the field can give your soon-to-be-job seeker some encouragement.

STRATEGY 3 – PREPARE
FOR CAREERS WHICH OFFER
EXPANDING JOB OPPORTUNITIES

Your youngster with special needs may have an interest in American literature, religious studies or art history, but I doubt, as fields of study, they'll offer a bright future in terms of a job market, unless one plans to become of a part of academia.

I recognize that there are individuals who consider their college years as a time for expanding their horizons, learning how to learn and "finding themselves." Yes, those activities are essential. And, taking those Liberal Arts college courses is helpful in gaining a well-rounded education.

Yet, as a person living with cerebral palsy, I've always wanted to know about the end game. When I was in college, I wanted to make sure I was doing everything I could (such as taking job-focused college courses) to prepare for the real world of work.

Maybe I was too competitive and too focused and passed up on soaking in some of the ambiance of college life. But, I knew it would be tough for me to get a job due to my cerebral palsy, and I worked diligently to prepare myself for employment -- taking what I thought were the "right" college course at the time and gaining a high grade point average.

I liked to write. So I chose journalism and advertising as a major and minor. I now see I was unknowingly preparing myself for business journalism, even though that field had not yet appeared in any labor department's list of occupations.

And, I had no idea, in 1965, that someday I would be a blogger. I believe it's difficult to predict what the "hot jobs" will be five years from now. If I were in college today, I'd be more open to "happenstance," the admission that even the most carefully crafted career plan can (and will) take strange and wonderful twists and turns.

Now that I've admitted my personal peculiarities when it comes to choosing a career and selecting college courses, I feel I can more freely recommend the following "job outlook" resources for your college student with special needs.

What Is Hot Right Now

Let us start from the perspective of college degrees. From that vantage point, one can then always look at individual college courses.

"As is typically the case, business and engineering majors, plus those earning degrees in technical fields, including computer science, are most in demand at the bachelor's degree level," writes the National Association of Colleges and Employers (NACE) in its "2012 Job Outlook."

While some studies break down which degrees are most popular nationwide, NACE's study is unique in that it polls employers and asks them to forecast their hiring intentions.

In 2011, NACE says, the five most in-demand bachelor's degrees, based on employer hiring intentions, were in accounting, finance, engineering, computer science and business administration (in that order).

For a larger perspective, check the occupations with the largest expected job growth from 2010 to 2020. Note that jobs in health care show the largest increases.

Additional career information is also available at America's Career InfoNet.

Top Resources

Here are five other resources I find useful:

- **A list** of the occupations projected to grow the *fastest* is available at www.bls.gov/emp/ep_table_103.htm.
- **Occupations** with the *largest* projected growth are available at www.bls.gov/emp/ep_table_104.htm.
- **A list** of ***industries*** with the fastest projected employment growth is available at www.bls.gov/emp/ep_table_203.htm.
- **The Office of Occupational Statistics** and Employment Projections home page at www.bls.gov/emp/ offers projected employment by occupation and industry.
- **The Occupational Employment Statistics** (OES) program (www.bls.gov/oes/) shows employment and wage estimates for more than 700 occupations for the U.S. as a whole as well as by state and metropolitan area.

For more detail about 250 different types of jobs, I recommend The Occupational Outlook Handbook. It's a nationally recognized source of career information, designed to provide people with valuable assistance in making decisions about work life.

The *Handbook* is revised every two years, and, for each job, it shows:

- Training and education (the college courses) needed
- Earnings
- Expected job prospects
- What workers do on the job
- Working conditions

In addition, the *Handbook* gives you job search tips, links to information about the job market in each state, and more. You can also view frequently asked questions about the *Handbook*.

For the *Handbook*, the Bureau of Labor Statistics develops projections only for the U.S. as a whole. Almost all states make projections for their states and some local areas. In addition, current employment data by occupation for states and areas are available from the Occupational Employment Statistics survey.

The *Occupational Outlook Handbook* is released in late March every other year.

The *Handbook* site contains virtually identical material to the print version. However, if you want a hard copy of the *Handbook*, ordering information is available from the Government Printing Office (GPO).

Remember that many of the new jobs on the horizon have not yet appeared in government publications. Instead of using these resources to pinpoint a specific job your college student may want to target, consider them as general guidebooks to the short-term future of work.

At any rate, from a longer point of view, having the right degree (based on current readings of the job prospects in your youngster's field) and understanding how that degree your youngster is working toward can best be leveraged in the job market are important factors in employment. That can help him or her be more attractive and competitive in the job market when the time comes to make the transition from school to work.

For instance, STEM careers are those which tap your youngster's capabilities in science, technology, engineering and mathematics (STEM) to levels much beyond what was considered acceptable in the past when we first encountered globalization and began to function as a knowledge-based economy.

Jim Brazell, technology forecaster and strategist who focuses on innovation and transformative systems, recommends this:

> Move from education which specializes in one or two of the STEM disciplines to a more systemic learning approach in which you can apply all four STEM capabilities (as well as the liberal arts you'll need in any work situation) across a variety of job sectors.

In other words, taking the right college courses now is often the key to getting hired later on. The feeling of "being of the right rack" can be a definite confidence booster.

STRATEGY 4 – DEVELOP THESE FOUR ESSENTIAL SKILLS

I've found that there are essentially four basic skills which can determine how successful a job candidate will be in landing a meaningful job: marketing, advocating, problem solving and negotiating.

Here's how I define each of those four essential skills.

Marketing

A huckster sells or promotes in an aggressive and flashy manner. A job seeker doesn't need to be a huckster.

But effective job seekers need to know the basics of personal branding. In today's American culture, which puts a premium on individuality, prime applicants for a job have identified their strengths and passion and packaged them into personal brands which showcase them in an effective, sincere manner.

Effective job applicants are objective about what they can offer an employer, even in the light of their special needs. They offer those attributes in a forthright presentation which puts the employer first and them second.

As a hiring manager today, I'd look for job candidates who have replaced the "objective" portion (which is "me" oriented) of their resumes with an "offering statement," which, in one sentence, tells prospective employers what they can do for them and their companies.

An offering statement is brief, reflecting a job applicant's well-selected accomplishments and skills. After all, an employer is more interested in what the candidate has to offer than what your college student's personal objectives are.

I call effective marketing the queen of these four personal development tools.

Advocating

Naked self-promotion is a negative in business circles. I want to hear what job applicants can do for my company or organization.

So, job candidates who happen to have a disability need to tell me, "This is what I need to do an effective job for you, and here's how I can help you get what I need at a reasonable cost and not a lot of time on your part."

I want a job applicant to be a self-advocate, and I want that individual to do it with the authenticity valued in today's business world.

At no time do I want a job candidate with special needs to beg for a job by falling back on the cliché of "all I need is just one break." People make their own breaks, disabled or not, by effectively preparing for a job, mastering effective job marketing techniques and showing employers why they are the best applicants for specific jobs.

Problem Solving

Imagination and daydreaming are fine pastimes, but what counts in business is creativity. Everyone can be creative, but not everyone is adept at applying creativity to personal challenges or on-the-job situations.

Problem solving is the ability to tap creativity for relieving a pain or paving the way to a gain -- either on a personal level or within a corporate setting. Ideally, your college student with special needs can demonstrate problem-solving ability in both areas.

For instance, I would want to know how applicants have harnessed technology to live well with their disabilities and how they can use that same ingenuity to adapt to my workplace requirements and help my company take advantage of often unseen opportunities.

Having that ability to match need and solution gives your college student with special needs the edge, in my mind, over any other applicant, regardless of disability. I want to hear brief stories which trace the evolution of an applicant's problem-solving abilities.

I believe personal-experience stories can be convincing evidence that a job candidate has devoted time and effort in cultivating problem solving in his or her bevy of key personal development tools.

Negotiating

Instead of approaching an employment opportunity as an underdog due to a perceived weakness, job candidates with special needs should possess basic negotiating skills so they approach decisions about employment conditions, benefits and salary from a position of strength.

After all, job candidates are selling their skills, experience and attributes, and, as the prospective employer, I'm buying them.

I want applicants who have taken courses in negotiation, read books about negotiation and have practiced their negotiating skills. Knowing (and demonstrating) how to negotiate effectively for what they want, need and deserve in terms of salary, benefits and accommodations will make them a stronger job candidate and a more effective employee.

In fact, I've found that job candidates who need accommodations are often savvy negotiators because they have had earlier-than-you-might-expect experience in identifying what they would like to have, what they'll likely get, what they need at a minimum and what is not acceptable to them.

Refining each of these skills (marketing, advocating, problem solving or negotiating) over the years will build self-confidence in the college student you're mentoring.

STRATEGY 5 – CONNECT WITH THE WORKFORCE RECRUITMENT POGRAM

According to the National Council on Disability's 2008 study, "Achieving Independence: The Challenge of the 21st Century," the most commonly cited reason among employers for not hiring people with disabilities is a "lack of qualified applicants."

Cornell University and the Workforce Recruitment Program (WRP) are proving that "not finding candidates with disabilities who are qualified and prepared" just does not have to be the case in this second decade of the 21st Century.

The WRP today is paving the way to brighter employment prospects for thousands of college students with a disability and access to new (and qualified) emerging talent for hundreds of employers across the U.S.

EARN at Cornell University Is a Key Connection

If your college student is finding it difficult to obtain a corporate internship, he or she needs to connect with the Employer Assistance and Resource Network (EARN) at Cornell University, the gateway to the WRP.

Since 1995, the WRP has provided employment opportunities for over 6,000 students with a disability, according to Kathleen Lee, business outreach specialist, Cornell University.

As a recruitment and referral initiative, the WRP connects federal and private sector employers nationwide with highly motivated post-secondary students and recent graduates with disabilities who are eager to prove their abilities in the workplace through summer or permanent jobs.

The WRP is co-sponsored by the U.S. Department of Labor's Office of Disability Employment Policy (ODEP) and the U.S. Department of Defense with the participation of many other federal agencies and sub-agencies.

What to Do

How does your college student get on the WRP's database? Here are a few things you need to know.

First, to participate in the WRP, your college student must be at least 18 years old and submit an online resume to EARN. Your college student's campus needs to have at least eight students with a disability apply for the WRP before a recruiter begins interviewing.

Second, contact the Disability Student Service (DSS) career counselor on your youngster's campus to make sure the school is a WRP participant. The WRP is currently working to expand its recruiting to more than 280 college and university campuses.

Third, to become a part of the WRP's annual database, your son or daughter needs to apply online at wrp.gov in *August of each year* in order to participate in the DSS training sessions on campus and meet with a disability-trained recruiter during October and November.

Candidates who qualify for the database are then contacted by EARN. The database is launched in December, and employers who complete an online request form can recruit students between December and July of the following year.

Fourth, candidates who become eligible for the database usually do well in both written and oral communication during interviews by a recruiter who understands disability employment issues.

Using a rating of 1 to 5, a recruiter evaluates each student applicant in terms of qualifications (based on transcripts, resume and experience), maturity, *written and oral communication (the "biggie")* and direction as well as an overall score. A student must score 3.0 or better in the overall rating to be eligible for the database.

Lee says the WRP offers advantages to both job seekers and employers during the recruitment process.

- **Job seekers, for instance, get the support** they may need to present themselves effectively during the database selection process. They are able to interview with a recruiter who understands disability. They are part of a recruitment process that offers a "level" playing field that engages employers who actively seeking job candidates with disabilities.

- **Employers feel more confident** that they are interviewing highly qualified students with disabilities as part of their overall recruitment strategies and that they have access to emerging talent. They have an opportunity to assess whether particular candidates are the "right fit" for their companies through an internship experience.

Help your college student with special needs take full advantage of the expanded opportunities he or she has through Cornell University by first researching EARN and the WRP.

The WRP provides another opportunity for your youngster to build self-confidence and to open doors in the mainstream workplace.

STRATEGY 6 – GET
A CORPORATE INTERNSHIP

Corporate internships are not free or cheap labor. They're not jobs. They're all about education. That's why there's frequently no pay for internships.

For your college student, internships provide practical, documented experience. By interning, he or she not only gains professional skills but also gathers insight into a particular industry or organizational culture and establishes connections that might lead to a job. That practical experience in a work environment supplements academic training.

For the employer, an internship offer a chance to see how your youngster works out in the position and as part of a team. It gives an employer a chance to observe your college student without having to commit to a new hire on a long-term basis.

So, help your college student approach an internship as part of his or her career preparation. That type of orientation is a career builder.

Paid summer internships are more common in certain fields and with specific types of organizations, according to internships.com. Private companies, large corporations, law firms, and real estate firms tend to offer paid corporate internships more often than not-for-profit companies or programs in the government sector.

However, many companies are becoming increasingly aware of the value of having educated, professional students intern with them, and, in return, they offer hourly wages or a stipend. Today there is also a broader realization that many college students, loaded with college loans, cannot afford to work for free.

Payment for a summer internship can be arranged in a variety of ways. Your college student may encounter installment payments or perhaps one payment of a lump sum based on the hours worked.

Help Your College Student Choose Well

Make sure you and your college student have investigated all the available options. Internships vary widely in the amount of pay or academic credit offered, the type of supervision and mentoring received, the length of time at work, and the amount of learning involved.

Study the requirements of the internship. Be sure your youngster has the fundamental skills, usually on the computer or on the telephone that the internship requires.

Beyond those basics, employers offering corporate internships look for students who are willing to discuss their work, have good listening skills, show politeness, are prompt and are responsible for their work. A sense of humor and a willingness to be flexible also help because both qualities show your college student knows how to work well with others.

Your college student may want to consider drawing up a "learning contract," which is a simple agreement outlining his or her goals for corporate internships. It provides a platform for agreement between both parties about what work your youngster will do and what supervision the company offering the internship will provide.

Your College Student Must Be Engaged as an Intern

As an intern, your youngster must approach an internship as an opportunity to work hard and learn. Without that approach, he or she will lose not only practical experience but also valuable references in the field.

So, your youngster must be eager and enthusiastic and ask for challenging work. He or she must be willing to take direction from the supervisor involved and take personal responsibility for carrying out duties which will make the internship productive for both intern and employer.

Encourage your son or daughter to tell his or her employer three things:

- "This is what interests me."
- "This is the type of work I'd like to do."
- "This is what I want to learn."

That helps the supervisor get a sense of your youngster's capabilities and adds new dimensions to the internship.

Your youngster needs to be personally invested in all the work, not just the fun assignments. He or she needs to ask a lot of questions to make sure assignment are being completed correctly.

Dealing with Special Needs as an Intern

From a disability perspective, corporate internships have an added value for both your college student and the employer involved. Here's what I would tell a college student with special needs:

"You have an opportunity to prove that you are capable of more than just meeting the basic qualifications. Your internship is your chance to prove to yourself and others that you have potential. And, by having a successful internship under your belt, you, as an eventual job seeker, provide uncertain prospective employers with a track record of successful work and assurance from another employer in their field.

"But, by helping spearhead a successful internship, you also are helping your employer show success in hiring and managing, even though temporarily, a person with special needs. You're actually breaking new ground for other interns and other job seekers with a disability who will follow in your footsteps."

Breaking new ground with an employer who is offering an internship to your college student with special needs is no small matter.

First, the employer may worry that the cost of an otherwise "reasonable accommodation" will be too expensive because of the temporary nature of the work.

A second concern, which is similar to the first but applies to non-disabled interns as well, is that the employer fears that the intern will take up too much supervision and training time that cannot be recouped in productivity during such a short stay.

Despite those two potential concerns on the part of an employer offering an internship, your youngster need not take the first internship offer on the assumption that he or she may not get another choice due to a personal disability. He or she deserves the same excellent opportunity as any other student in competing for corporate internships.

Here are three more bits of advice about corporate internships I'd share with your college student:

- "Let your employer know that, other than your specific disability, you have the same abilities as all others. Your disability will not affect your work or prevent you from being a good team member.
- "You may have to work harder than other interns to overcome some of these employer concerns, but always be cautious about asking for extras not directly related to your disability and be above reproach.
- "And, communicate (verbally and non-verbally) with confidence. In short intern relationships, there is no time for hand holding. In terms of accommodations, tell the employer what you will need, and then prepare to find an alternative way of dealing with it if you can't get it."

One more tip: Pass along these two excellent references for finding internships among disability friendly companies to your college student: gettinghired.com and wrp.gov.

A successful internship, even after college graduation, can increase your youngster's morale and confidence.

STRATEGY 7 – KNOW
WHICH INTERVIEW QUESTIONS
COMPLY WITH THE ADA

Your college student may have had recent job interviews which involved discussions about disability with prospective employers that he or she believes were not appropriate under the Americans with Disabilities Act (ADA).

But neither of you may not be aware about what is accepted and what is not under the Equal Employment Opportunity Commission (EEOC) guidelines.

Here's a quick set of fair, questionable and unfair job interview questions, based on the EEOC guidelines, which you and the college student you're mentoring can use as indicators about whether an interview experience is on the up-and-up or dipping below the fairness (and illegal) level.

Always remember that the EEOC enforces the employment provisions of the ADA according to the following provisions.

Unacceptable Application or Interview Questions

- "Do you have a physical or mental disability which would interfere with your ability to perform this job?"
- "Have you been hospitalized recently?"

- "How many days were you sick last year?
- "Have you ever filed for worker's compensation?"
- "Have you ever been injured on the job?"
- "What prescription medications do you currently take?"

Under Title I of the ADA, a job applicant can't be asked about the existence, nature, or severity of a disability.

It prohibits questions about medical conditions, past hospitalizations, nature and severity of disabilities, and other related matters on job applications and in job interviews.

The ADA, however, does not require employers to give your son or daughter preference just because he or she has a disability.

The law prohibits an employer from refusing to hire or promote or from taking other adverse action against a person because of the person's disability, if he or she can *perform the essential functions of the job*. It applies to private employers with 15 or more employees and to state and local government employers.

An employer can, under the ADA, choose a person without a disability with more experience over an individual with a disability, even if the individual with the disability is qualified for the job.

An employer can choose a person without a disability over an individual with a disability, if the two individuals are equally qualified, as long as the choice was not made because of the individual's disability.

The ADA prohibits employers from asking questions that are likely to reveal the existence of a disability before making a job offer (the pre-offer period). This prohibition covers written questionnaires and inquiries made during interviews as well as medical examinations.

However, such questions and medical examinations are permitted after extending a job offer but before the individual begins work (the post-offer period).

Employers may ask an applicant these questions after making a job offer as long as they ask the same questions of other applicants offered the same type of job. In other words, an employer *cannot* ask such questions only of those who have obvious disabilities.

Similarly, an employer may require a medical examination after making a job offer as long as it requires the same medical examination of other applicants offered the same type of job.

An employer may tell all applicants what the hiring process involves (for example, an interview, timed written test, or job demonstration), and then ask whether they will need a reasonable accommodation for this process.

If the employer believes an applicant with an obvious disability will need a reasonable accommodation to do the job, it may ask the applicant to describe or demonstrate how she would perform the job with or without reasonable accommodation.

A Fair Question under the EEOC Guidelines

- "Can you perform the basic functions of this position with or without accommodation?"

An employer may ask you whether you can perform the job-related functions as long as they don't phrase the questions in terms of the disability.

For example, if driving a vehicle is a function of the job, the employer may ask if your college student has a driver's license. However, the employer may not ask if your job seeker has a visual disability that would prevent him or her from driving.

A "Questionable" Question under the EEOC

- "Why is there gap in your employment history between 2005 and 2007?

Under the ADA, potential employers cannot ask certain questions at a job interview that would result in the applicant revealing information about the existence or nature of a disability.

Questions about gaps in employment history are likely to lead to information about an applicant's disability and are arguably illegal. However, at this writing, the law on this question is unsettled.

How to React to Unacceptable Questions

Unfortunately, despite wide dissemination of the EOCC guidelines, some employers persist in asking questions that are prohibited under the ADA. This places job applicants such as your son or daughter with special needs in the uncomfortable position of deciding how to respond.

My recommendation to pass along to your college student: Try to determine what type of information an employer is looking to receive with such prohibited questions.

For example, an interviewer asking about children and their ages may be trying to find out if an applicant would likely be missing work to care for them. The job candidate might simply answer, "I will have no problem meeting the position's attendance requirements."

In deciding to pursue a job despite questionable interview questions under the EOCC guidelines, your son or daughter may choose to simply refuse to answer certain questions in a non-confrontational manner.

For instance, your job seeker could state, "I read about a law that prohibits questions of this type during job interviews." Such a response avoids answering the question and avoids the discussion about disability.

If the main goal is to get the employer to change the illegal interview process, then filing a detailed complaint with the EEOC or state or local human rights agencies is appropriate.

At any rate, your soon-to-be job seeker needs to study the EOCC guidelines, be able to recognize when job interviewing is going off on the wrong track and know how to respond effectively. That will increase his or her self confidence in launching a job marketing campaign.

STRATEGY 8 – ASSESS A PROSPECTIVE BOSS'S LEARNING PREFERENCE

Once your college student starts getting into second and third interviews with prospective employers, he or she needs to quickly ascertain the hiring manager's approach to interpersonal communication and how that person prefers to learn and process new information.

Knowing that preference will give your youngster tips about how to complement that style with a presentation in which both individuals feel "we're on the same wave length."

Getting to that simpatico feeling requires that your college student:

- **Recognize** how that hiring manager is using a particular learning style during the interviewing process.
- **Adjust** his or her presentation style so it matches more succinctly the hiring manager's learning preference because the goal is to help that decision maker internally process information quickly and easily.

Four Learning Styles

A learning style normally involves these considerations:

- How did you learn to study?
- Do you learn more easily by reading, watching or hearing material?
- Do you work best in a quiet environment or with some background noise?
- Do you work better independently or in groups?

An individual's learning style also depends on one's likes, dislikes, and abilities when it comes to reading, public speaking, memorizing, summarizing, problem solving, analyzing, interpreting, and reviewing.

In her research about personality types, Susan Dellinger, Ph.D., has identified several communication styles she says we all tend to use in certain circumstances. However, most individuals, she believes, follow one or two of the communication styles as a predominate pattern. And watching for certain cues, she maintains, can help us identify which communication mode a person is currently using.

After studying Dellinger's communication research findings and those of others since 1990, I have used my 29 years of experience in corporate communications to identify four learning styles in terms of how people tend to process information within the world of work:

The "focused" individual:

- Learns from first-hand experience, using all five senses.
- Is logically organized.
- Focuses on ideas and tasks and how they affect the bottom line.
- Thinks methodically and predictably but also relies on gut instinct.

The "analytical" individual:

- Is persuaded by logical reasoning, impersonal analysis and systematic planning.
- Is concerned more about ideas than people.
- Needs time to decide and adjust to change.

The "nurturing" individual:

- Relies more on what people say than technical analysis.
- Wants to know how people feel about various options.
- Relies on experience and intuition to make decisions.

The "creative" individual:

- Thrives on change.
- Makes quick decisions.
- Bases opinions on the feelings of others.
- Generates ideas easily.

CEOs of companies or administrators of organizations tend to be "focused" individuals. We'll likely find "analytical" individuals in the legal or finance departments or in the information services section. "Nurturing" individuals gravitate to jobs in public relations, sales training and human resources. We can expect "creative" individuals in the corporate communications and advertising groups.

These generalizations, of course, are vastly over-simplified. People are more complicated than that. We usually see a complex mix of styles in every occupation. A hiring manager can switch from one communication style to another (just like your son or daughter does).

From my vantage point, these learning styles can help your son or daughter communicate effectively with a hiring manager about a crucial topic -- an on-the-job accommodation plan, for instance, during a second or third job interview with the same employer:

The "focused" individual:

Since this individual is logically organized and thinks methodically,

- Present evidence in an orderly fashion with goals and objectives first.
- Focus on ideas.
- Be brief and concise.

- List pros and cons of each alternative within the accommodation plan.

The "analytical" individual:

Since this individual is persuaded by logical reasoning, impersonal analysis and systematic planning,

- Present details before the "big picture."
- Show practical and realistic applications.
- Focus on personal experience with other accommodation plans.

The "nurturing" individual:

Since this individual wants to know how people feel about various options,

- Present points of agreement first and then the points of known contention.
- Support ideas with stories about previous accommodation experiences.
- Be willing to use trial and error to find the right answer.

The "creative" individual:

Since this individual bases her opinions on the feelings of others and generates ideas easily,

- Present the broad issues first.
- Offer novel and unusual ideas about how the accommodation can be implemented.
- Speak to her instincts.

Remarks from the hiring manager such as "I get your drift," "That's on target" etc. show your college student is connecting and communicating with the hiring manager.

If your youngster hears, however, a response such as "Let me think about it," the hiring manager may just be in an "analytical" mode or have something more pressing on her mind. Or your youngster may not be connecting at all, and she's confused and doesn't want to admit it.

Your youngster, of course, may not be able to determine which is really happening until the final outcome: he or she gets hired.

That's one small example of why interpersonal communication is an art -- and not a science -- and why those who know how to communicate well (and recognize various learning styles) within the workplace will always be in demand in the job market.

Why Learning Styles Are Important

Your son or daughter also gains a couple of important benefits by methodically using learning styles to quickly build a rapport with a prospective supervisor, who is usually involved in the hiring process and the final decision maker. Your youngster will probably:

- **Be able** to work out problems with that supervisor more easily -- even sticky ones such as harassment from a co-worker or a sticky accommodation request.
- **Assimilate** into the organization more quickly and more completely.
- **Be** more productive in his or her work.
- **Have** more opportunity to use his or her skills on the job and acquire new ones.
- **Gain** a sense of appreciation and security based on accomplishment in a work world that is anything but secure.
- **Enjoy** work.
- **Be setting** a good example others in the company can cite for hiring other individuals with special needs.
- **Be demonstrating** effective interpersonal skills, which are essential and valuable in today's job market.
- **Be establishing** a foundation for a mentoring relationship with the supervisor and for improved personal development and promotion opportunities.

STRATEGY 9 – JOIN
A MASTERMIND GROUP

In 2008, an instructor introduced me to the concept of using a "mastermind" group to help me actually put into practice what I was learning through his online course about building a business on the Web.

Based on that personal experience, I began asking myself, "How can individuals with disabilities tap that spirit of working together toward a common goal to gain insight from others about obtaining meaningful employment?"

After all, I had been certified as a Global Career Develop Facilitator (GCDF) just three years earlier (in 2005) and had developed an online course, "Online Networking as a Job Search Tool" in 2007 for eSight Careers Network.

I'm now thinking about a process for career counseling that is more focused, more personal and much smaller (in terms of number of members) than a "job club." Let me explain by pointing out the need, purpose, guidelines and potential of a "mastermind" group.

The Need: Obtaining Honest Feedback from Others

In many fields today, expertise is thought to be not a static condition but one that is built and sustained through feedback from others. Coaching in pro sports, for instance, holds that, no matter how well prepared people are in their formative years, few can achieve and maintain their best performance on their own.

Good coaches know how to break down performance into its critical individual components, according to Atul Gawande in his October 3, 2011, article, "Personal Best" in the New Yorker magazine.

"You have to work at what you're not good at," writes Gawande. "In theory, people can do this themselves. But most people do not know where to start or how to proceed... The coach provides the outside eyes and ears and makes you aware of where you're falling short."

Richard N. Bolles is author of "What Color Is Your Parachute?" He says we, as individuals, don't often see clearly who we are -- that we sometimes don't recognize our strengths, our weaknesses, and our potential.

We need honest feedback from others to clearly see all three. Bolles recommends job seekers work in teams of three to five people to discover what is not always easily evident. I believe we can meet that need by harnessing the "mastermind" concept for effective career counseling online.

For your future job seeker with special needs, that means collaborating with others in a personal dialogue and figuratively sitting in front of a mirror to find who each participant can be -- a process which can help each discover their work barriers and how they can work around them.

The Purpose: Giving and Accepting Support

When three to five people (including your college son or daughter) who are willing to mentor and support one another come together and engage in dialogue for that purpose, you have the beginnings of a "mastermind" group.

Your college student needs to find "mastermind" members who have a common purpose in mind: finding meaningful work. Those members need to be willing to coordinate knowledge and effort, in a spirit of harmony, to achieve that purpose.

More specifically, each member needs to approach all "mastermind" meetings with these two goals in mind:

- *Give:* Gladly provide support, encouragement and feedback to each other.
- *Accept:* Graciously receive support, encouragement and feedback from others.

In doing so, the members of a "mastermind" group build a safe environment in which to share their dreams, desires and goals; find solutions to their challenges; build self-esteem; develop strong relationships with one another; tap into resources they may not have discovered on their own; and become more accountable for reaching their goals.

By directing this "giving and accepting support" purpose toward "finding jobs that are right for us," your soon-to-be-job seeker can have a powerful career counseling experience.

The Guidelines: Establishing a "Mastermind" Group

Your college student can start a "mastermind" group by collaborating on a statement of purpose and an understanding of how members want to operate as a group. Here are some essential guidelines for doing that:

Select a facilitator for the group so all meetings can run smoothly. Rotate that function among members so eventually everyone has an opportunity to share in that responsibility.

- **Bring** solutions instead of problems to the table.
- **Understand** that everyone in the group will support one another.
- **Agree** that each meeting will start on time and absences must be highly unusual.

Who should your college student invite to be members of his or her group? Start with people he or she knows: college classmates, professional association members, LinkedIn members etc.

Remember, ideal members are people who want to work within a group to help accomplish great things for each member. A group of future job seekers, for instance, may want to experience career counseling online and step through the job hunting process and have an ongoing agenda for helping each other find their individual ways to:

- **Identify** personal interests and strengths.
- **Match** skills and aptitudes with appropriate jobs.
- **Showcase** personal accomplishments.
- **Conduct** company research.
- **Frame** disability as a competitive edge.
- **Do** well in job interviews.

What media are available to the group? Use telephone conferencing, Skype, Goggle Hangouts, real-time text chat or in-person meetings. The medium is not as crucial as the guidelines for interactivity that group members choose to follow.

Explore potential "mastermind" guidelines for setting up a group geared toward career counseling online.

I believe few people who achieve a meaningful goal do it alone. Throughout history, for most of these "achieving" people, a group of like-minded individuals (perhaps in gatherings we just happen to call "mastermind" groups in the 21st. Century) have provided the critical guidance and leverage for achievement through the exchange of ideas.

That's where you, as a parent, coach or mentor, can be helpful for your college student with special needs. You are his or her mentor and now may be the time to extend that mentoring through a "mastermind" group structured around getting a job.

STRATEGY 10 – DEVELOP EMOTIONAL INTELLIGENCE

Emotional intelligence (EI) has a surprising relationship to success in a business setting. MetLife, for instance, has found its sales associates who score high in EI outsell those with low EI by an average of 37 percent during their first two years of work.

Your college student with special needs probably possesses EI skills, but they may be under-developed and an untapped resource. A youngster is not born to do well on an emotional intelligence test. EI is learned (unlike an individual's intelligence quotient) -- first from you, as a mom or primary caretaker, and then from others, such as a mentor.

So, exactly what is an emotional intelligence test? Here are some characteristics you have probably already recognized in yourself as a parent, mentor or coach:

- **You are resilient** to stress, enabling you to very rapidly calm and refocus yourself under trying circumstances, according to Jeanne Segal, Ph.D., a psychologist, sociologist, popular speaker, and internationally recognized author. For instance, she says, you use gentle humor to help you say things that might be difficult without creating a flap and use appropriate eye contact, facial expression, tone of voice, touch, posture and gesture to show you're paying attention to others.

- **You have the potential** to identify your own and someone else's emotions and feelings, you use these emotions and feelings in constructive ways, you can sense someone else's complex feelings that he wishes to conceal and you can crack a joke and cheer others on a team by saying the right thing at the right time, says Carlos Todd, LPC.

- **You form optimal relationships** with other people through the attributes of hope, empathy, trust, integrity, honesty, creativity, resiliency, consequence-thinking and optimism so you can build stronger social networks and manage difficult situations, write J. S. Stein and H. E. Book in "The EQ Edge: Emotional Intelligence and Your Success" (Jossey-Bass, Hoboken, N.J., 2006).

- **You see the positive side** of stressful situations and empathize with the less fortunate, states study team leader and psychologist Robert Levenson, University of California-Berkeley.

I'm reminded of this quote from Aristotle at around 350 BC:

> "Anyone can become angry; that is easy. But to be angry with the right person, to the right degree, at the right time, for the right purpose, and in the right way -- that is not easy."

Aristotle knew about emotional intelligence before EI became a buzz word.

But, the two most intriguing characteristics of EI that I've found are these (again from J. S. Stein and H. E. Book): the ability to delay gratification in pursuit of long-range goals and the ability to "unlearn" helplessness and hopelessness when faced with adversity.

What You Can Do

Guide your college student with special needs in learning how to get in tune with his or her EI. You may ask: "How has learning to deal effectively with your disability helped you acquire and build your EI?"

Then, encourage your youngster to develop a brief narrative which illustrates that connection. Discuss how it can be applied to a prospective employer's circumstances.

That brief story, used strategically during a job marketing campaign, can help your college student successfully make the transition from school to work -- and find the right job with the right employer.

STRATEGY 11 – DEMONSTRATE LEADERSHIP

One of the marks of leadership is how flexible your college student with special needs is in working with people to effectively get a job done as an employee, coworker or supervisor.

For me, that flexibility means knowing when to step up, when to step aside and when to step down on the job for the benefit of the corporate endeavor. As a hiring manager, I want to know that a job seeker has the self-confidence, self-knowledge and social intelligence to first think about the general good of the work group or project instead of a particular self-interest.

That's not especially easy to pull off, especially in today's American society, which rewards individual initiative and discounts company loyalty as a career building attribute. First thinking of the general good was also once a mark of statesmanship and leadership, but the global stage is now populated with political and business figures who don't know how to step up, step aside or even step down.

This leadership issue of serving the greater good through temporarily suspending your self-interest gets even more complicated when you have a disability. Consider these questions:

- **When** is it constructive for an employee with special needs to step up, step aside or step down?
- **How** do you decide when your disability is limiting your flexibility to serve the greater good?

- **When** are you being too passive and feeding into stereotypes your supervisor or coworkers may have about people with disabilities?
- **When** does such a move discount you instead of reward you as an individual? When does it show you as a strong leader instead of a weak link?

Let's address these questions by citing concrete situations which you can pass along to the college student you're mentoring.

Here are some personal stories I would be prepared to tell during job interviews to illustrate my self-confidence, self-knowledge, social intelligence and dedication -- key attributes in the leadership potential hiring managers seek in today's job candidates.

Stepping Up: Volunteer to Take a Pay Cut

At one point in my career, I volunteered to take a 60 percent in my salary to save my job at a non-profit. It was the right thing to do at the time because funding was not forthcoming and I was one of the highest paid members of the small full-time staff.

Looking back, it turned out to be good decision. The non-profit survived five more years, and I ended up working full-time as its employee for another year and then as an independent contractor for the agency during another four years.

In that instance, I had the financial resources to take the pay cut. I gained credibility among coworkers and board members by stepping up to help the non-profit deal with its financial crisis and achieve some of its immediate key objectives.

Stepping aside: Grant Exceptional Authority to Staff

About 15 years into my career, I made the transition from "doer" to managing my team of staff members who carried out the "doer" work. I learned how to develop job descriptions, conduct evaluations and delegate authority to individuals on my team based on their unique capabilities.

As a person with CP, I talk and walk with difficulty. So, during a 24-year span, I had an opportunity to refine my team of "doers" and attracted some of the most accomplished individuals in corporate communications (about 36 professionals in all) by offering them the opportunity to gain recognition of their efforts (tasks I could not do as well) while I stayed in the background as a people manager.

In short, I developed my own leadership style.

Stepping Down: Develop a Career in a New Field

Reporting to our CEO as vice president for corporate communication, I could finally see the end game of more than 20 years of mergers within the Midwest dairy industry: a consolidation of three large dairy processors (including our own).

Our CEO was spear-heading this final round of restructuring across five states, and I knew he had a problem. He needed slots in his top-management team for the CEOs of the other two organizations, and corporate communications (administered by someone who could not speak very well due to CP) and human resources (a recently developed function) were the obvious slots.

He warned me that the upcoming two years would be rough and offered me the opportunity to create any job for myself within the upper management structure at a generous compensation package, if I would step aside and let one my trusted staff members take over temporarily as vice president during the transition period.

I tried to introduce an organizational development function within the company but decided to retire after a year to start my own business because I realized my services were more needed elsewhere --- in disability employment. And, an additional year later, the expected consolidation fell into place, and corporate communication merged with human resources under one vice president.

It was a good 29-year ride for me within one organization, but, with my disability, I realized I could not compete for a position that was targeted by so many other heavy hitters. Instead, I stepped down and over another two decades reinvented myself into a disability employment expert (anchored in my original leadership style).

As a job seeker, your college student mentee may have similar stories which could come in handy during job interviews when he or she needs to prove levels of maturity, trustworthiness, dedication -- and a lack of self-centeredness -- to a prospective supervisor.

That supervisor is probably asking in the back of his or her mind:

- Is this candidate realistic about the limitations disability may have in the job at hand?
- Is this person willing to not only serve the corporate good but also accommodate to the realities of the job and of personal limitations?
- Is this person going to require more of my time and effort than usual in helping him or her adjust to the changing realities of the job?

Urge your college student to tell brief stories about his or her previous experiences which address those concerns about leadership.

Remember, such stories can stem from not only previous work experience but also volunteer positions as well as interactions with caregivers and experiences while in college.

Such stories can be powerful in illustrating your mentee's leadership, a competitive edge honed through learning how to live well with a disability.

STRATEGY 12 – RECOGNIZE THE IMPORTANCE OF A RESUME'S OPENING STATEMENT

It doesn't matter whether your college student's resume is scanned by a machine or a real person during the initial phases of a recruitment process. In either case, the most important part of his or her resume is the opening statement.

There are basically three options for opening a resume: objective statement, summary statement and offering statement. Developing any one option can be the toughest part of writing a resume.

Here's how to explain those three resume writing options to your college student:

- An "**objective statement**" explains, usually in one sentence, what you're seeking in a job as a job applicant. It briefly describes your personal interests.
- A "**summary statement**" tends to go into more detail and communicates what you can bring to the table in terms of the job at hand.
- Like an "objective statement," an "**offering statement**" is also very short. It says, "This is what I can do for you." It helps you focus your job marketing plan on meeting your targeted employer's needs.

Let's look at each of these resume writing options in more detail. As a mentor, I would explain each to my college student mentee like this:

Objective Statement

Showing an objective can convince employers that you know what you want to do and are familiar with the field.

"Stating your objective on your resume is optional -- having an objective for your resume is not; you need to be clear about your employment goals," writes Alison Doyle, a job search expert with many years of experience in human resources, career development, and job searching.

If you include an objective on your resume, Doyle points out, it's important to customize your resume objective to match the position you seeking. The more specific your resume objective is the better chance you'll have of being considered for the job.

Here is a sample resume objective statement:

"Obtain a position within the pulp paper industry where I can maximize my management skills and experience in quality assurance, program development, and training."

Summary Statement

A summary statement can quickly and effectively brand yourself to a prospective employer, according to Dana Leavy, founder of Aspyre Solutions career coaching in New York, which helps young and mid-level professionals find their way through the process of career transitions and launch effective job search strategies.

Highlight your most relevant strengths, skills and core competencies that are unique to you as a candidate, versus a trait or skill that's an industry or professional standard (i.e. "multi-tasker" or "team-player"), says Leavy.

The summary statement should be approximately four to six lines and speak to your professional background only, according to Leavy. Do not address any outstanding circumstances (employment gaps, change of career, personal experiences etc.). A cover letter is an expanded version of the statement.

Here is a sample summary statement:

"Hands-on executive officer with extensive experience in food processing industry recognized nationally for planning, developing, implementing and measuring corporate-wide internal and external marketing and branding communication programs designed to align corporate goals with stakeholder interests, resulting in long-term stability and growth."

Note that, in the above example, the candidate touched on the following elements, all of which are key to effective resume writing:

- Core strengths and skill sets most relevant to his or her role.
- Past relevant experience with key functions.
- Notable accomplishments that they intend to repeat in the next role.

Offering Statement

Blogger Mary Ann offers this recommendation about the focus of your resume's opening statement:

"Replace the typical 'objective statement' that begins pretty well every resume with an 'offering' statement.'

The former is 'me' oriented, and the latter is 'employer' oriented. An 'offering statement' is brief, reflecting well-selected accomplishments and skills of the job applicant, using action words. An employer is more interested in what an applicant has to offer than what the applicant's personal objectives are."

Mary Ann's resume writing observations coincide with what Nick Corcodilos, the headhunter, maintains. In his book, "How Can I Change Careers?," Nick writes:

"...Go back to your past accomplishments. What skills did you use? Make a list of those skills to help you think about them. How did each accomplishment help your company become more successful or profitable? It doesn't have to be a huge difference that you made, but it has to be a difference that contributed to the bottom line. Now take those skills and ask yourself, 'How would I apply them to solve the problems and meet the challenges of the companies I want to work for?'

"...It takes a lot of work to develop this kind of statement. You have to learn a lot about the company you are pursuing, including exactly what kind of specific help a particular manager needs."

Mary Ann's "offering statement" is what Nick calls a "value offered" statement. I call it an "offering statement."

A well-written offering statement is easy and quick to present and pass along to the right decision maker.

Here is a sample resume offering statement:

"I will enhance your company web site's usefulness as a marketing channel by developing it as a gathering place for those within your niche disability audience who seek

opportunities to discuss issues which are important to them."

In this example, the job seeker is marketing a service designed to meet a need for a specific person within a particular company -- a service that only he or she can best provide. That targeted employer could be the marketing manager of a company which is trying to promote its particular line of adaptive technology for workplace situations through a static web site.

An offering statement is like a summary statement for a business plan. Like an offering statement, a summary statement in a business plan often succinctly defines what value a proposed project has for potential investors. In an offering statement, you're briefly describing what value (specific benefits) you offer your potential supervisor.

You can often use your offering statement outside of your resume and portfolio. It can come in handy when you are updating your profile in LinkedIn, Facebook, Twitter or any other social networking situation.

In all three resume writing approaches, the upfront statement is often the first item read, so that statement must get to the point by essentially saying, "Here's why you should hire me."

By following that formula, regardless of which resume writing option used, your college student will be a step ahead of other candidates competing for the same job.

STRATEGY 13 – FOLLOW THESE TIPS ABOUT HOW TO LAND A JOB

"Almost half of all working-age people with disabilities in America today are employed," writes Elisabeth (Harney) Sanders-Park, president of WorkNet Solutions, Riverside, CA.

"That's nearly 20 million people, and you can join them," she adds. "Employers will choose you, if you can prove you can solve a problem, make them money or help them be more successful. But, you must prove that your disability will not become their problem."

And, she asserts, "For every barrier you have, there is someone who has faced it, overcome it, and is working today."

And, here are a couple of figures about the economy Sanders-Park cites in "The 6 Reasons Why You'll Get the Job" (Prentice Hall Press, 2010), a book for job seekers which she co-authored with Debra Angel MacDougall:

> Despite high unemployment numbers during the worse period of what is now the Great Recession (January 2009), more than four million people got jobs and one million jobs were unfilled in the U.S.

Sanders-Park and MacDougall also wrote "No One Is Unemployable: Creative Solutions for Overcoming Barriers to Employment" (WorkNet Training Services, 1997), a book for career counselors hailed as "Top 10 Career Book of the Year" by the Los Angeles Times.

Neither book is about disabilities per se, but they both include sections specifically for job seekers with disabilities.

I first became acquainted with Sanders-Park's "No One Is Unemployable" book as a Global Career Development Facilitator (GCDF) student in 2005 and met her at the 2011 Careers Conference, Center on Education and Work, University of Wisconsin-Madison, where she was a presenter.

Four Essential Steps

Here are my disability-slanted "takeaways" from her 2011 Careers Conference presentation and "The 6 Reasons Why You'll Get the Job," which she co-authored.

Sanders-Park says, to a land a job in any economy, your college student needs to take these four steps:

- **Clarify** the job target by pinpointing the available opportunities.
- **Prove** you can do the job by showcasing your attributes, skills and values.
- **Avoid** getting screened out and make it to the second interview by using keywords throughout the hiring process that show a good match between qualifications and the employer's stated needs.
- **Get** in front of the people who have the hiring authority by using networking strategies (either in person or through social media) that will tap the hidden (unpublished) job market.

To tap the hidden job market, today's job seeker does not need to be involved over the whole range of social media that are available in the current online environment.

A more effective networking strategy may be to select one medium that best meets one's needs, hone a personal profile on that medium and then ride with it, learning the "ins" and "outs" of that particular community.

As a job seeker, I've found that LinkedIn or Twitter (or a combination of the two, using Twitter to search for open jobs and using LinkedIn to build relationships with individuals working in targeted companies) can be the best avenues.

But, let's look at point number 3 (above) more closely. As a job seeker with special needs, your son or daughter can easily be screened out early on in the hiring process either automatically by a computer program or by someone on staff who is not the final decision maker.

How to Get to Decision Makers

To avoid be screened out before the second interview, your college student needs to develop a workable strategy that best fits the situation -- a strategy which will give him or her an opportunity, as Sanders-Park puts it, to "show your skills are more valuable than your perceived 'costs' (in terms of accommodations etc.)."

In other words, a prospective employer must have some reason to reduce her or her initial perceived risk in hiring your son or daughter with special needs.

Specifically, Sanders-Park suggests job seekers with disabilities consider these strategies:

- **Target** jobs you are fully qualified to do with your particular disability.

- **Structure** your job search so employers see your value before they notice your disability.

- **Decide** whether and how to disclose your disability.

- **Avoid** words and imagery that could intensify employer concerns. For instance, I use "some difficulty in muscle control" instead of "cerebral palsy or CP" in describing my unusual condition, since "cerebral palsy" can conjure up images about me that can go way beyond reality.

- **Reduce** your prospective employer's perceived risk by presenting solutions for "resources that will help me be more productive" (more preferable, Sanders-Park writes, than "accommodations") so the employer can refocus on your abilities.

But, that's only part of the process of getting hired.

Six Transferrable Skills

In "The 6 Reasons Why You'll Get the Job," Sanders-Park details, from an employer's perspective, these six transferable skills she says your new job seeker will need to illustrate in concrete terms in order to get hired:

Appropriate presentation
- Do you look, sound and act like the employer?
- Will you represent the employer in a positive way?

Matching attitude
- Do you fit the company culture?
- What's your outlook on work?
- Do you show flexibility and respect others?

Dependability record
- Will you work for the company's best interests?
- Will you be loyal to the company?

Personal motivation
- Will you help the company achieve its goals?
- Are you demonstrating that you'll mirror the company's values?

Basic trainability
- How well will you apply your abilities to the job at hand?
- Can you learn and adopt?
- Can you produce results quickly?

Valuable network
- Do you have access to people who will benefit the company?
- Will your online contacts reflect positively on the company?

The candidate who is hired for a particular job usually stands out in all six areas, Sanders-Park maintains -- and (this is especially important for your college student with special needs) those six areas need to outweigh any perceived risks the employer may have about hiring a person with disability.

To further tip that benefit-risk balance in your son or daughter's favor, I'd offer proof that he or she can meet the employer's needs in a positive way. Here's how I would frame that suggestion for your college student:

> Tell a story that is not more than 60 seconds long which shows you acting positively in a work situation. Your story needs to demonstrate that you have the attributes the employer values. Your story should include numbers or percentages to quantify your accomplishment. In other words, show what the employer will specifically gain by selecting you for the job.

Sanders-Park even suggests that your student start networking with someone in the targeted company's HR department or a present employee via LinkedIn or by telephone to further clarify what the employer values in an employee.

"You're then in a position to show and tell about how you match those needed skills throughout the hiring process," she notes, highlighting the importance of company research as a part of a job search.

In fact, I view all of these tips as parts of an overall job marketing template for your soon-to-be job seeker – one that can provide him or her with a competitive edge.

Discovering Disability's Competitive Advantage

STRATEGY 14 – BECOME A SAVVY JOB HUNTER

Here are 20 lessons I've learned during my years in business about employee recruitment that may make the transition from school to work a little bit smoother for your college student.

I believe launching a career when special needs are involved takes a lot of savvy and hard work. Let's sidestep the "hard work" aspect of your son or daughter's new venture and focus here, instead, on the "savvy" part.

For me, being savvy about how to find a job when you have special needs means:

- **Realizing** that being treated with dignity is a universal right of any job seeker, disabled or not.
- **Recognizing** that going into business for yourself, which requires experience, is not often a viable alternative to competing for a job once you're ready to make the transition from school to work.
- **Knowing** the difference between disability-friendly, inclusive employers and EEOC-driven employers who simply seek to qualify for state and federal government contracts and knowing how to find a job within each type of company.
- **Admitting** employers are not responsible for "giving you a chance" as a job applicant; learning how to find a job is your responsibility.

- **Learning** the difference between prejudice and bias and how to effectively address each as a job seeker.
- **Highlighting** your ability to deal effectively with ambiguity as a personal attribute in your job marketing campaign.
- **Selling** yourself as a bridge builder who can help your prospective employer prepare for upcoming shifts in the employee landscape, where older, sometimes disabled workers become more prevalent.
- **Turning** the negative perception of dependency into an advantage as a job candidate with special needs.
- **Positioning** your personal approach to vulnerability as a standout attribute during job interviews.
- **Using** authenticity to put your prospective hiring manager at ease about your disability.
- **Describing** your volunteer experience so it's meaningful to hiring managers.
- **Making** sure you're in the right line when recruiters visit your college campus.
- **Showing** hiring managers you'll bring an entrepreneurial spirit to their work teams.
- **Moving** beyond self-absorption about your disability to a mainstream orientation.
- **Reassuring** your prospective hiring manager you know how to avoid being an "easy mark" at work."
- **Learning** how to gracefully accept and decline help at work and in public.
- **Being** clear about your career ambitions upfront with prospective employers.
- **Showing** a prospective employer how your resiliency will contribute to the company's bottom line.
- **Putting** job interviewers at ease about accommodations you may need to be effective at work.
- **Knowing** your rights under the Americans with Disabilities Act (ADA) – and those of your prospective employer.

So, here's my message to the college student and soon-to-be job seeker you're currently mentoring:

"As you visit with the hiring manager at a specific employer for an open job that feels right for you, cite examples of how learning how to live well with a disability has given you measures of maturity and authenticity not normally found in other job candidates within your age group."

That's leveraging disability's edge.

STRATEGY 15 – TAP
THE HIDDEN JOB MARKET
THROUGH LINKEDIN

Your soon-to-be-job-seeker college student needs to tap social media to the fullest extent possible to show employers he or she has innovative ideas, valuable contacts and a bottom-line focus. Let me explain why I believe that is so.

Using social media appropriately is actually another way to extend one's education. It's an avenue for lifelong learning and networking.

Jack Chapman, founder of Lucrative Careers, Inc., hosted a January 13, 2011, webinar presentation by Jason Alba, CEO of JibberJobber.com ("Your Personal Relationship Manager") and author of "I'm on LinkedIn - Now What???"

In setting the stage for Alba's remarks, Chapman, who has personally assisted more than 2,000 individuals, one-on-one, in improving their careers, pointed out this paradox:

> Today's "published" job market has 33 percent of all available jobs and 100 percent of job seekers, but the "hidden" job market has 66 percent of all jobs but just five percent of job seekers.

During a recession, that hidden job market is even more pronounced because employers with open jobs don't always publish them. They don't want to deal with hundreds of applicants, Chapman points out.

To tap the hidden job market, your college student needs to network -- to connect with the right person for the right job at the right time, according to Alba.

And, the various social media are godsends for soon-to-be-job seekers with special needs because they make networking much easier and time efficient.

Here are the online tools Alba uses to navigate the hidden job market:

1. Blogs
2. Twitter
3. LinkedIn
4. Facebook
5. Article submissions to blogs and e-zines
6. Newsletters

He repurposes his content for each of these tools and then cross promotes in the various social media. But, he uses LinkedIn as his focal point and emphasizes that effectively working with its Profile, Questions/Answers, Groups, Companies and Advanced People Search functions is crucial in a job search.

Surprisingly, I've had career counselors on campus tell me that many college students don't maintain a presence on LinkedIn while they are in school. Instead, they tend to wait until graduation to get serious about networking on LinkedIn.

By using LinkedIn, your college student can connect with exactly the right people in the companies where he or she wants to work.

I recently ran across this comment from Boris Epstein, the CEO and Founder of BINC (AskBinc.com), a professional search firm that specializes in the software marketplace:

> "Nowadays employers rarely hire just skills and are looking for much more of a complete package -- skills plus a well-rounded individual that fits well with their team and company. And a person's social media footprint gives employers (and others) the best insight into your passions, interests, communication styles, work habits, work/life balance and all sorts of other valuable information.

"Simply put, it helps an employer get to know you and get comfortable with you before a single word has even been exchanged. So think about it -- if you had the choice to consider a cold, bland resume or an actual person with common interests, passions and work/life style, wouldn't the choice be obvious?"

If your youngster doesn't know anyone in a targeted company, LinkedIn provides the opportunity to find connections who can introduce him or her to a key contact within the company or to one of their connections who can make the introduction. Replicating that social network gives a new dimension to career networking, company research, and job marketing.

College students with a well-established social network have one advantage over the pre-Internet job candidates who relied on in-person "informational interviews" to build their networks. That advantage is this: People in social networks want to connect with others and establish relationships. That's why they are there.

They may have a research or selling objective in mind, but most understand that meeting that objective comes as a result of cultivating genuine relationships by being helpful to others (answering questions, offering information, and making introductions).

In doing informational interviews in the 1990s, I often felt like I was intruding on someone's time during business hours, even though I was sincerely trying to learn about the person's job.

That's not the case with social media, which have been developed precisely for networking.

That means your college student can confidently put his or her best foot forward in a social network setting. Coach your youngster to describe what he or she we needs in a concrete, authentic way — always remembering to help others in the same way.

Building a robust network on LinkedIn while in college (and being "ahead of the game" upon graduation) may prove to be your soon-to-be job seeker's competitive edge, especially if he or she can develop relationships with hiring managers who have had good outcomes in hiring people with special needs.

STRATEGY 16 – CONSIDER A GOVERNMENT JOB

Here's why I believe both federal and state government jobs, although they may not be as secure as they once were given the current economic and political climate, are still viable options for your youngster with special needs:

> Government agencies can be gateways into mainstream employment for people with disabilities because they are often in the forefront of leveling the recruitment playing field for people with special needs.

Federal and state government jobs are good employment options for your college student because they offer a wide variety of exciting work environments, good wages, and medical benefits. And they offer applicants the opportunity to make a difference through public service.

Federal Jobs

Let's first examine government jobs at the federal level. Here's a quick fact sheet you can share with your college student:

How do I become a federal employee?

There are three ways to get into the federal service.

- You can serve as an intern first – check www.wrp.gov.
- You can be hired competitively.
- You can be hired non-competitively (Schedule A).

Where do I find out about federal government jobs?

Most federal vacancies are advertised on the USAJOBS website, where you can search for openings in a particular field, city, agency, or all three.

Note, however, that some agencies do not use USAJOBS to advertise vacancies, so always check specific agency websites for additional information on employment opportunities. A listing of agency sites can be found at www.usa.gov.

What is Schedule A. Am I eligible to use it?

Schedule A is a non-competitive hiring authority available for federal agencies to hire and/or promote individuals with disabilities. By using Schedule A to fill a vacancy, an agency can avoid using the traditional, and sometime lengthy, competitive hiring process.

You are eligible for a Schedule A appointment if you are a person with a severe physical or mental disability.

How do I prove my eligibility for Schedule A?

In order to receive a Schedule A appointment, you must:

- Be qualified for the job you are applying for (*i.e.*, have the necessary knowledge, skills and abilities to perform the required duties).
- Demonstrate "proof of disability."
- Be job ready.

Proof of disability can be satisfied with a simple letter stating that you have a severe disability. You can get this letter from your doctor, a licensed medical professional, a licensed rehabilitation professional, or any entity that issues or provides disability benefits.

The letter does NOT need to detail your medical history or your need for an accommodation. Simpler is better.

Individuals with a disability who opt to apply for a job through Schedule A -- a hiring authority allowing agencies to appoint a qualified, disabled applicant to a position without competing with the general public -- were previously required to produce a "certificate of readiness" from a medical professional or rehabilitation specialist, stating the individual could perform the job.

In February 2013, the Office of Personnel Management (OPM) removed this "certificate of readiness" requirement to be consistent with President Obama's call to strip barriers to hiring people with disabilities into the federal workforce.

The OPM now states it is confident managers can use standard procedures when interviewing you to ensure you are qualified for the job.

State Jobs

Most states also have level-playing field initiatives when it comes to recruiting and hiring individuals with disabilities, although they don't offer the federal non-competitive Schedule A hiring authority, which is exceptional.

For information about what initiatives your state offers in helping individuals with disabilities compete for government jobs, go to disability.gov/employment#map.

For example, in Wisconsin candidates with a disability who apply for a civil service position with Wisconsin State Government can participate in the *Disabled Expanded Certification* (DEC) program.

DEC is a special affirmative action program which gives persons with disabilities an increased opportunity to be interviewed for jobs in state government.

To be eligible for the DEC program, a candidate must have a permanent physical or mental impairment that substantially limits the major life activity of working. This means that the person's disability significantly restricts his or her ability to perform a class or broad range of jobs when compared to the average person who has comparable training, skills and abilities.

Wisconsin also provides special accommodations to job seekers with disabilities to enable them to take civil service examinations. Those accommodations include readers, writers, large print exams, sign language interpreters, and other accommodations depending on the needs of the applicant.

In some cases, Wisconsin may even waive examinations for individuals with certain disabilities where one's qualifications for the job cannot be adequately measured by a standard civil service exam.

I believe you'll find similar provisions in the state where your college student with special needs applies for state government jobs.

The bottom line: making the best use of the incentives for hiring individuals with disabilities in federal and state government can give your soon-to-be job seeker an important edge in today's job market.

SUMMARY

Preparing for a meaningful career as a college student with special needs can seem overwhelming at times. But, as a career-coaching parent, you can help your soon-to-be job seeker do just that by focusing on these key strategies:

Growing in Self-confidence

Strategy 1: Use These Guidelines to Choose a Career Counselor – Selecting the right career professional for your soon-to-graduate son or daughter is a step toward enhanced self-confidence.

Strategy 2: Heed Rehab Counselor Survey Results - These little bits of insight from those in the field can give your soon-to-be job seeker some encouragement.

Strategy 3: Prepare for Careers Which Offer Expanding Job Opportunities - Taking the right college courses now is often the key to getting hired later on. The feeling of "being of the right rack" can be a definite confidence booster.

Strategy 4: Develop These Four Essential Skills - Refining each of these skills (marketing, advocating, problem solving and negotiating) over the years will build self-confidence in the college student you're mentoring.

Strategy 5: Get a Corporate Internship - A successful internship, preferably before college graduation, can increase your youngster's morale and confidence.

Strategy 6: Connect with the Workforce Recruitment Program - Help your college student take full advantage of the opportunities to build self-confidence and to open doors in the mainstream workplace through the WRP.

Strategy 7: Know Which Interview Questions Comply with the ADA - Your soon-to-be job seeker needs to study the EOCC guidelines, be able to recognize when job interviewing is going off on the wrong track and know how to respond effectively. That will increase his or her self confidence in launching a job marketing campaign.

Strategy 8: Assess a Prospective Boss's Learning Preference - Once your college student starts getting into second and third interviews with prospective employers, he or she needs to quickly ascertain the hiring manager's approach to interpersonal communication and how that person prefers to learn and process new information.

Discovering Disability's Competitive Advantage

Strategy 9: Join a Mastermind Group – As your youngster's mentor, now may be the time to extend that mentoring through a "mastermind" group structured around getting a job.

Strategy 10: Develop Emotional Intelligence - Guide your college student in learning how to get in tune with his or her emotional intelligence. You may ask: "How has learning to deal effectively with your special needs helped you acquire and build your emotional intelligence?"

Strategy 11: Demonstrate Leadership - As a job seeker, your college student probably has stories which could come in handy during job interviews when he or she needs to prove levels of maturity, trustworthiness, dedication -- and a lack of self-centeredness -- to a prospective supervisor.

Strategy 12: Recognize the Importance of a Resume's Opening Statement - The upfront statement in a resume is often the first item read, so that statement must get to the point by essentially saying, "Here's why you should hire me." By following that formula, regardless of which resume writing option used, your college student will be a step ahead of other candidates competing for the same job.

Strategy 13: Follow These Tips about How to Land a Job – They are parts of an overall job marketing template for your soon-to-be job seeker – one that can provide him or her with a competitive edge.

Strategy 14:- Become a Savvy Job Seeker - There are 20 lessons I've learned during my years in business about employee recruitment that may make the transition from school to work a little bit smoother for your college student.

Strategy 15: Tap the Hidden Job Market Through LinkedIn - Building a robust network on LinkedIn while in college (and being "ahead of the game" upon graduation) may prove to be your soon-to-be job seeker's competitive edge, especially if he or she can develop relationships with hiring managers who have had good outcomes in hiring people with special needs.

Strategy 16:- Consider a Government Job - Both federal and state government jobs, although they may not be as secure as they once were given the current economic and political climate, are still viable options for your youngster with special needs because of the extra leverage they provide job seekers with disabilities.

I wish you much success in carrying out these 16 key career-building strategies for your college student.

NATIONAL CAREER DEVELOPMENT GUIDELINES

According to the National Career Development Guidelines (NCDG), these are the competencies your son or daughter should be developing at the "implementation" level during college:

Valuing one's personal interests, likes, and dislikes as a step toward building and maintaining a positive **self-concept**.

Practicing respect for **diversity** as an essential positive interpersonal skill.

Anticipating growth and **change** as essential parts of career development.

Achieving a **balance** among personal, leisure, community, learner, family and work roles.

Acting on the premise that **educational** achievement and performance levels are needed to reach personal and career goals.

Committing to ongoing, **lifetime learning** as a means for enhancing one's ability to function well in a diverse and changing economy.

Creating and managing a **career plan** for meeting career goals.

Making **decisions** within an overall personal strategy for managing a career.

Using accurate, current and unbiased **career information** in planning and managing one's career.

Accumulating consistently the fundamental knowledge about the variety of **skills** that are important for success and advancement in school and work, such as communicating, critical thinking, and problem solving.

Analyzing changes in employment **trends**, societal needs and economic conditions and the impact they have on one's career path.

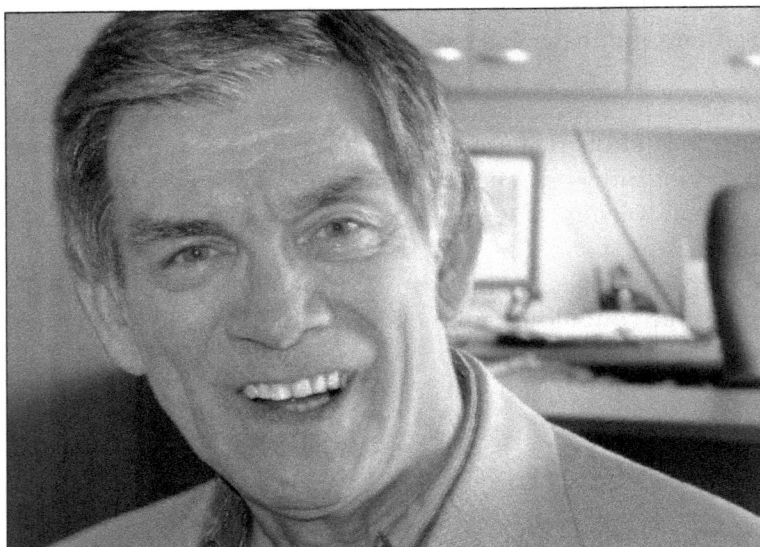

ABOUT JIM HASSE, THE AUTHOR

Jim Hasse is the founder of <u>cerebral-palsy-career-builders.com</u>, the comprehensive career coaching guide for parents of CP youngsters 7 to 27 years old.

He owns Hasse Communication Counseling, LLC, which helps champions of disability employment form partnerships for win-win direct mail fundraisers.

As a Global Career Developmental Facilitator (GCDF) since 2005, he's the author of 12 Amazon eBooks, each of which explains his central premise: that disability, when framed correctly, can be a competitive advantage in today's job market for job seekers with special needs.

To access his books in electronic as well as soft-cover formats, see <u>http://tinyurl.com/JRH-All-Books-Amazon</u>.

JIM BOOKS

7 TRANSFORMATION STORIES

**Quick Career-insight Series of Seven Little Books
for Parents of Youngsters with CP**

Each of the seven Little Books takes about 40 minutes to read. Each illustrates and summarizes the essential career builders for your youngster's age group – all through seven transformational stories about Jim Hasse's personal experience as a person with CP.

You'll find considerably more detail about each career builder at cerebral-palsy-career-builders.com, which can be used as an ongoing reference for "how to" information as your youngster matures.

7 TRANSFORMATION STORIES

Little Book 1 (Career-coaching Series) about Self-confidence
FOR PARENTS OF ELEMENTARY STUDENTS
with Cerebral Palsy

JIM HASSE

Buy **Little Book 1** on Amazon
at- http://www.amazon.com/dp/B00DPLHRTI

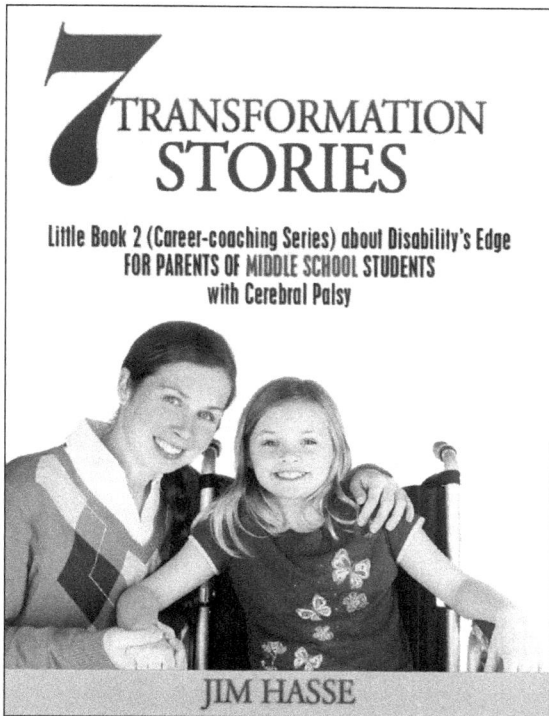

Buy **Little Book 2** on Amazon
at http://www.amazon.com/dp/B00H9WAKHA

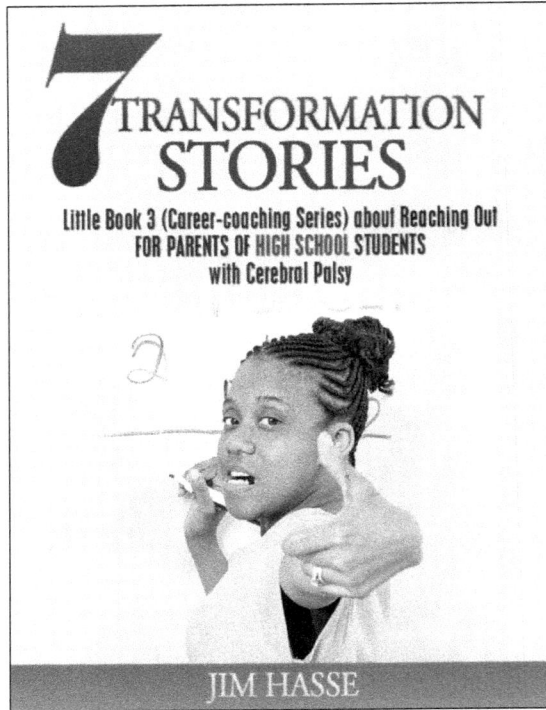

Buy **Little Book 3** on Amazon
at http://www.amazon.com/dp/B00HB77RAQ

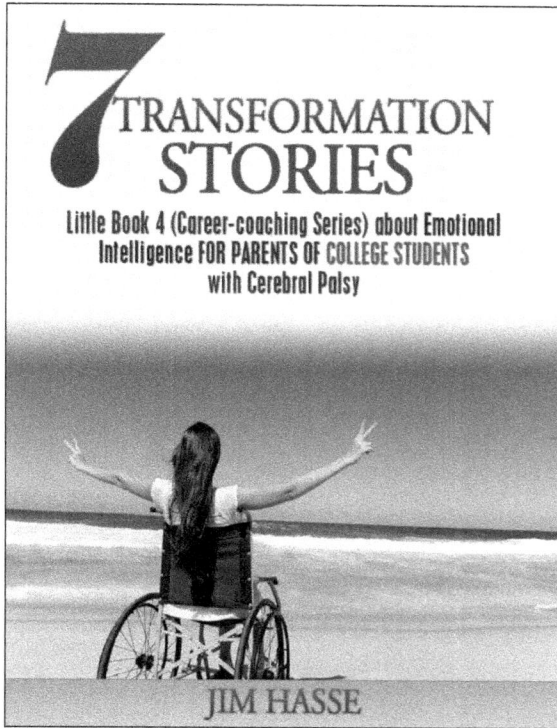

Buy **Little Book 4** on Amazon
at http://www.amazon.com/dp/B00HBDUJ96

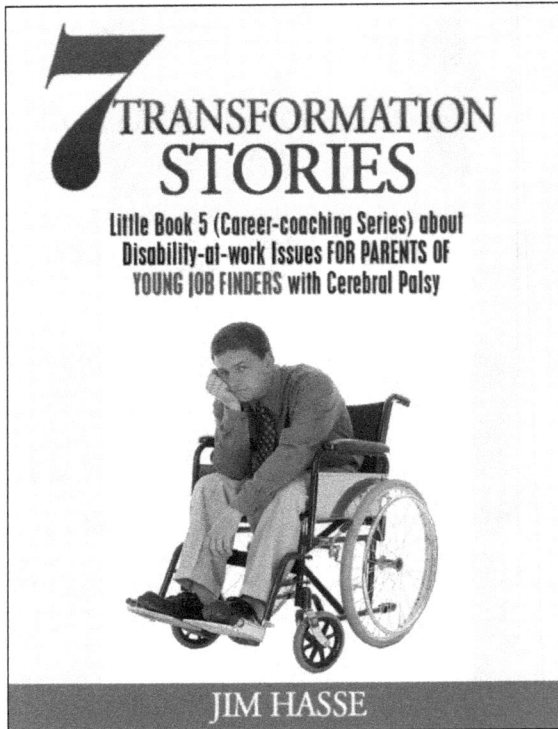

Buy **Little Book 5** on Amazon
at http://www.amazon.com/dp/B00HBVTZ02

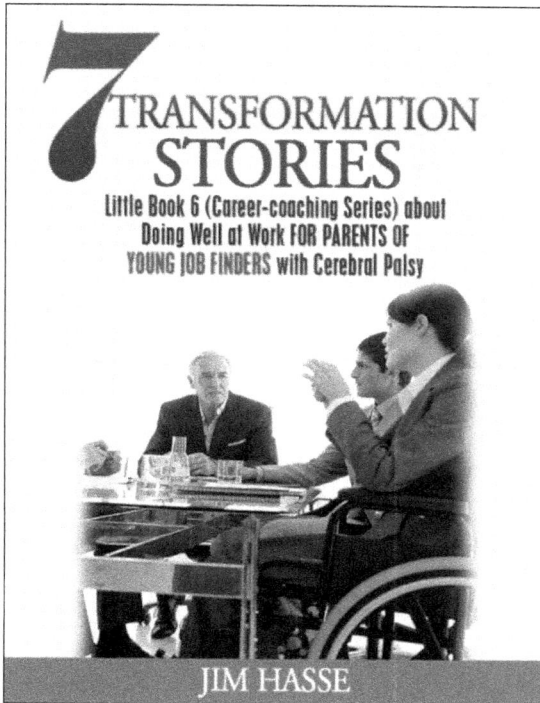

Buy **Little Book 6** on Amazon
at http://www.amazon.com/dp/B00HE60J8G

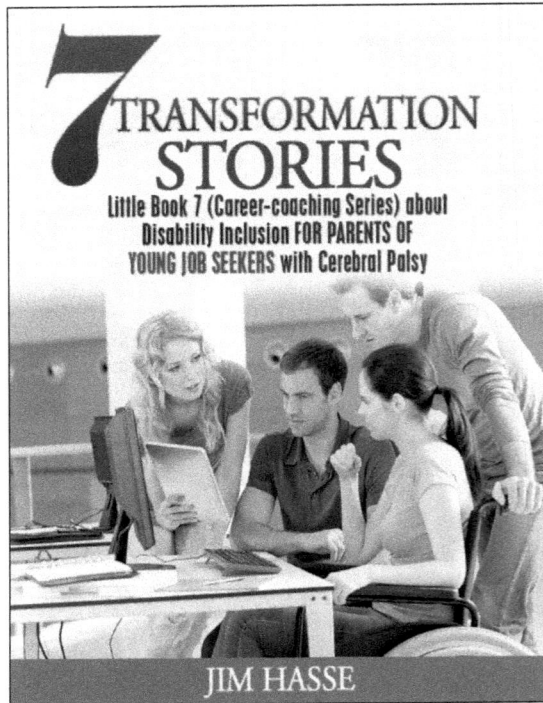

Buy **Little Book 7** on Amazon
at http://www.amazon.com/dp/B00HEVJYUU

Five Books *for* Parenting Youngsters with Special Needs

CAREER BOOK

Each of these five books (available in electronic and paperback formats) takes about 40 minutes to read. Each illustrates and summarizes the essential career development strategies to follow for your youngster's age group – all based on the roadmap recommended by National Career Development Guidelines (NCDG) and Jim Hasse's experience as a Global Career Development Facilitator and as a person with cerebral palsy and mainstream work experience.

You'll find considerably more detail about each career building strategy at www.cerebral-palsy-career-builders.com, which can be used as an ongoing reference for "how to" information as your youngster matures.

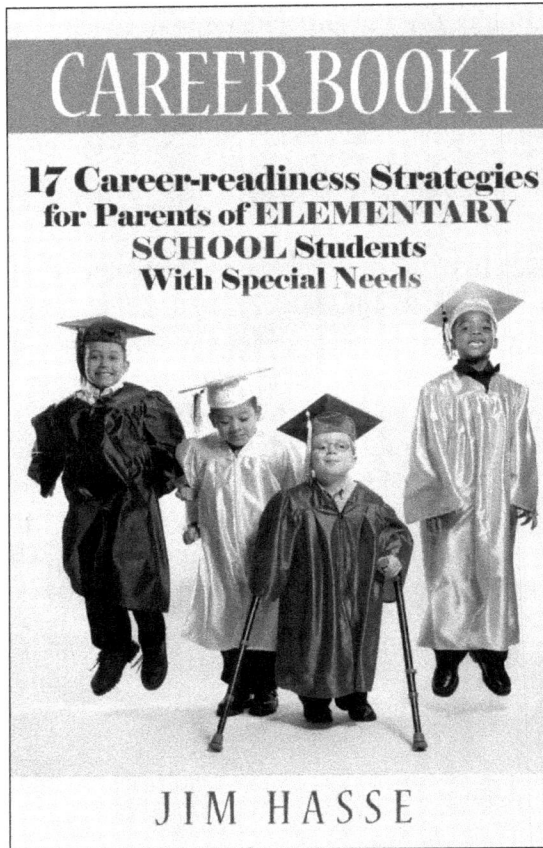

Buy **Career Book 1** on Amazon
at http://www.amazon.com/dp/B00JNYH6JM

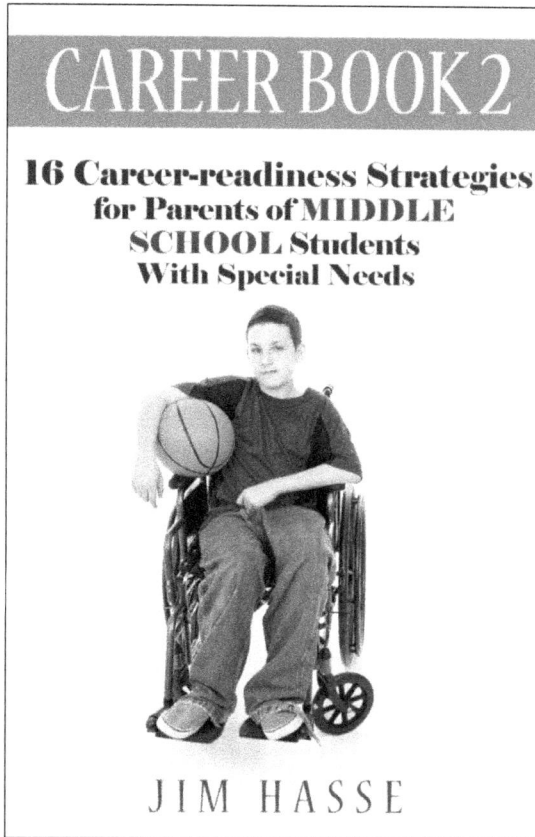

Buy **Career Book 2** on Amazon
at http://www.amazon.com/dp/B00KLIMPBS

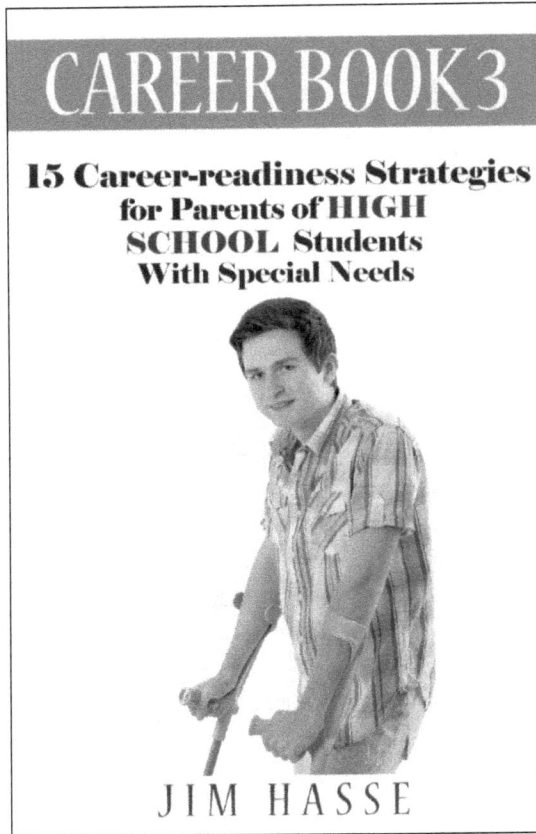

Buy Career Book 3 on Amazon
at http://www.amazon.com/dp/B00KN2OF56

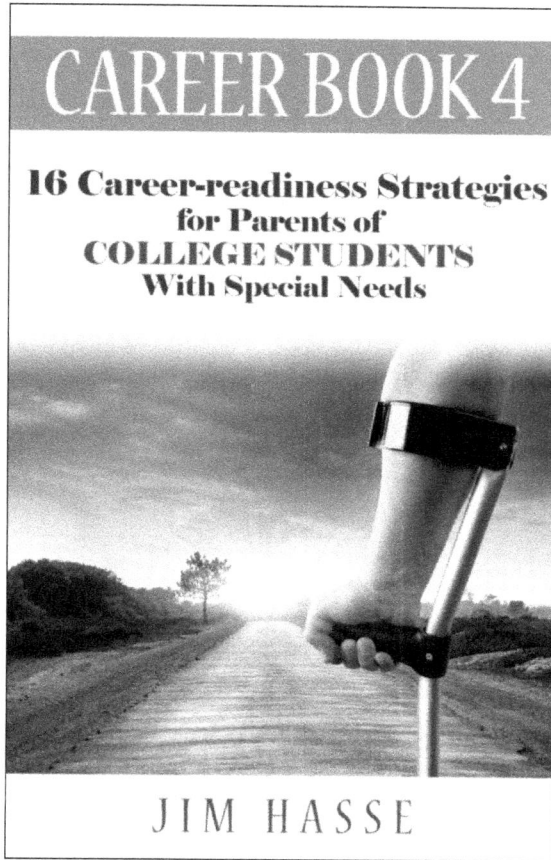

Buy **Career Book 4** on Amazon
at http://www.amazon.com/dp/B00KPGV5B2

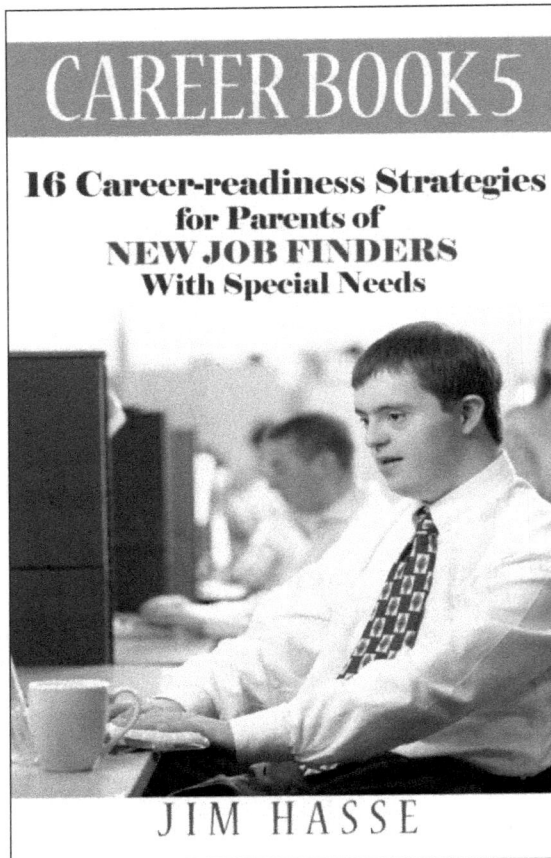

Buy **Career Book 5** on Amazon
at http://www.amazon.com/dp/B00KQRZIHC.

www.ingramcontent.com/pod-product-compliance
Lightning Source LLC
Chambersburg PA
CBHW060954040426
42445CB00011B/1155